Mapping in the Modern World

MAPPING
HUMAN
ACTIVITY

Tim Cooke

Crabtree Publishing Company
www.crabtreebooks.com

Crabtree Publishing Company
www.crabtreebooks.com
1-800-387-7650

Published in Canada
616 Welland Ave.
St. Catharines, ON
L2M 5V6

Published in the United States
PMB 59051
350 Fifth Ave. 59th Floor
New York, NY 10118

Published in 2017 by CRABTREE PUBLISHING COMPANY

Author: Tim Cooke

Designer: Melissa Roskell

Cover Design: Katherine Berti

Picture Manager: Sophie Mortimer

Design Manager: Keith Davis

Editorial Director: Lindsey Lowe, Kathy Middleton

Editor: Janine Deschenes

Children's Publisher: Anne O'Daly

Proofreader: Ellen Rodger

Production coordinator and Prepress technician: Ken Wright

Print coordinator: Margaret Amy Salter

Produced by Brown Bear Books for Crabtree Publishing Company

Photo credits

Photographs (t=top, b=bottom, l=left, r=right, c=center)

Front Cover: Wikimedia Commons: inset second, third, and fourth from left; All other images from Shutterstock

Interior: Alamy: Chromepix.com 24; Bill Rankin: 8, 29b; Catherine Linard: 11; DETROITography: 27; Doug McCune: 14; Eric Fischer: 13t; Flowminder.org: 10; Fritz Freudenheim: 29c; Google Inc.: 9t, 9b; Heinrich Berann: 26; inhabitat.com: 28; innovative GIS: 7b; Jeremy Wood: 29t; Kate McLean: 15; Library of Congress: 12, 13b; NASA: 20; New York Times: 5; NOAA: 1, 19, 21, 22, 25b; Shutterstock: Andrey Popov 23; USGS: 18, NASA/NPS 17; Wellcome Library, London: 4, 6; Wikipedia: 7t, 16, 25t.
All other photos, artwork and maps, Brown Bear Books.

Brown Bear Books has made every attempt to contact the copyright holder. If you have any information please contact licensing@brownbearbooks.co.uk

Library and Archives Canada Cataloguing in Publication

Cooke, Tim, 1961-, author
　　　Mapping human activity / Tim Cooke.

(Mapping in the modern world)
Includes index.
Issued in print and electronic formats.
ISBN 978-0-7787-3222-8 (hardcover).--
ISBN 978-0-7787-3240-2 (softcover).--
ISBN 978-1-4271-1883-7 (HTML)

　　　1. Human geography--Juvenile literature. 2. Cartography--Juvenile literature. I. Title.

GF48 C66 2017　　　j304.2　　　C2016-907115-4
　　　　　　　　　　　　　　　　　　　　　　　　C2016-907116-2

Library of Congress Cataloging-in-Publication Data

CIP available at the Library of Congress

Printed in Canada/052017/TL20170327

Contents

HUMAN BEHAVIOR

Modern maps are a useful way to record and **visualize** human behavior. They reveal patterns that help understand and predict how people act.

Maps can record a huge range of information about humans. Almost any sort of **data** about people can be represented visually on a map. For example, **cartographers** can represent where different groups of people live in an area, such as people who speak certain languages or follow certain religions. They can also map where most people die in the hospital, or where in a city or country supporters of rival sports teams are more likely to live.

In 1889, Charles Booth mapped London, England's wealthy homes in gold and red colors, and poorer homes in blue. His map showed exactly where the wealthy and poor lived within the city.

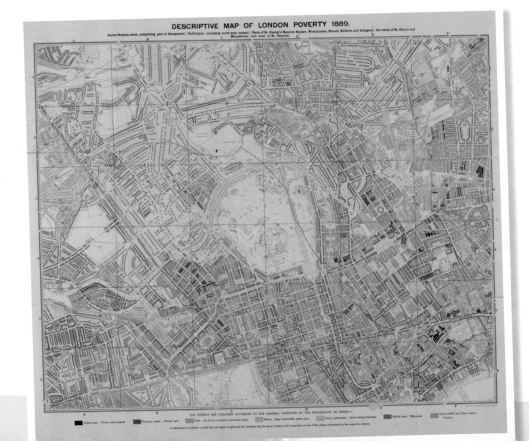

DESCRIPTIVE MAP OF LONDON POVERTY 1889.

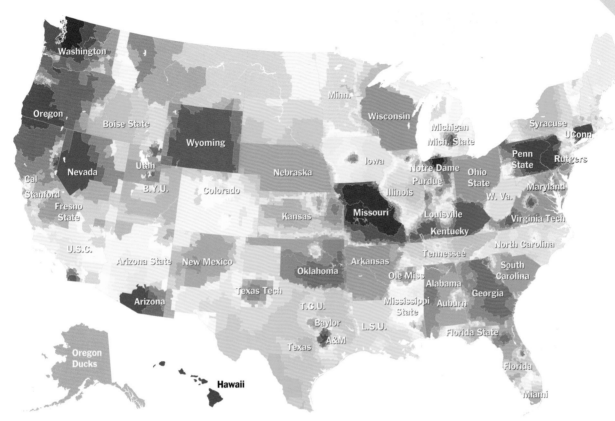

This map shows areas of strong and weak support for U.S. college football teams. Each color represents the named team. The bolder shades of each color show areas of strongest support, with lighter tones of the color showing weaker support.

Visualizing Statistics

Maps that represent human activity are sometimes called behavioral maps. These maps are usually based on **statistics**. Since the middle of the 1800s, governments and other organizations have kept statistics, or records of human activity. These statistics are often difficult to interpret. It is not always possible to see patterns or trends from lists of figures. Representing statistical information in visual form on a map makes it much easier to understand.

Maps are powerful tools. City councils can use them to identify the road intersections with most traffic accidents, for example, or areas with poorly performing schools. Governments can use them to record things such as areas with many immigrants.

The Map that Helped Cure Cholera

In 1854, a severe outbreak of cholera occurred in the center of London, England. Cholera, a deadly infection, was assumed at the time to be caused by "bad air." Trying to find the cause of the infection, a physician named John Snow made a map of the area. He marked all the houses where people were sick or had died. In the middle of the area was Broad Street. Snow realized that the sick people had all used the water pump in the street. To test his discovery, Snow had the handle removed, so the pump could not be used. The cholera stopped spreading. Snow had discovered that cholera was caused by dirty water.

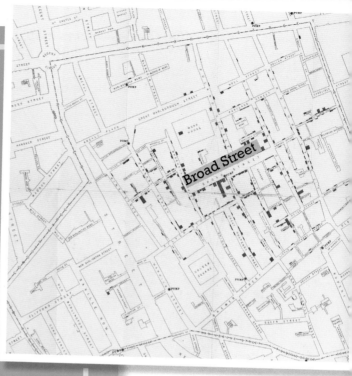

Broad Street

John Snow's map of cholera cases was the first example of using mapping to identify the source of an infection.

This information can be used to decide which areas need more social services, or where funding, or government money, needs to be given to help people. Doctors can see places where cases of infectious diseases have broken out. Retail chains, or groups of many stores, can map the amounts and types of goods that are sold from each store. By doing so, they can make sure each store has enough of the right goods in stock. Fire and police departments can also map areas to figure out where to concentrate their **resources**. For example, fire departments will make sure that an area that is at-risk for wildfires will have a lot of fire-fighting resources.

Did You Know?

Maps of human behavior show one of two types of data. Some maps illustrate quantities of things, such as how many supporters a football team has. Other maps shows things that are not quantities, such as the locations of teams. Some maps use both methods together.

On Charles Dupin's map of France, darker shading indicated the areas of least education. They were also among the poorest areas of the country.

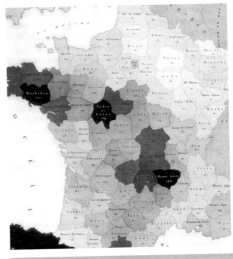

Showing Data on Maps

Maps have been used to visualize and display information about people since the 1800s. In 1826, Charles Dupin drew a map of the regions of France. To show how many boys attended school in each region, he shaded the regions dark for many school attendees and light for few attendees. Dupin was trying to figure out the link between **literacy** and wealth. His map clearly showed that the poorest regions of France had the worst numbers of boys who attended school, therefore having the lowest literacy. Dupin's map persuaded the government to build more schools in the areas with the lowest literacy, to help poorer people have better opportunities for education.

This map of a large retail store shows routes with the most footfall. Yellow and red indicate the routes that most people take through the store.

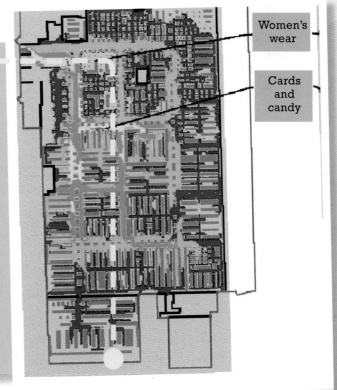

Women's wear

Cards and candy

In the Real World

The Department Store Route

Have you ever noticed that when your family goes to a department or grocery store, you follow roughly the same route through the aisles? Stores do a lot of analysis of the routes shoppers take through their aisles. They analyze where shoppers are most likely to stop and pick up items. That helps them figure out how to arrange their shelving. They make sure that the best-selling items and new promotions are positioned along the routes most shoppers use.

Dupin's map is called a **choropleth**—the first of its kind. Choropleths are maps that display information by figuring out average statistics for an area. These averages are colored according to a key, a scheme in which colors or shades represent different information. Dupin's experiment was influential. Many **social reformers** began to map aspects of people's lives. They used patterns revealed by the maps to urge governments to help those in need.

A Modern Variation

Choropleth maps are now widely used. A modern example is the map created by the US academic Bill Rankin in 2010, which showed where ethnic groups live in Chicago. He used a technique called dot density. Dot density is a type of map that uses map dots to represent things. Using data from the U.S. **Census**, a national survey that records population numbers and personal information, Rankin added a color-coded dot for every 25 people of a particular race who lived in a city block.

Variable Data

Information for modern maps is gathered from a wide range of sources. Some cartographers use government statistics or data from stores. Others use tracking information from cell phones to map how people move around. Mapmakers compiled the information they needed to create the football map on page 5 by recording mentions of college football teams on Facebook.

Bill Rankin's map shows where people who identify as different **races** or **ethnicities** live in neighborhoods of Chicago. The key on the right side shows which colors represent each race or ethnicity.

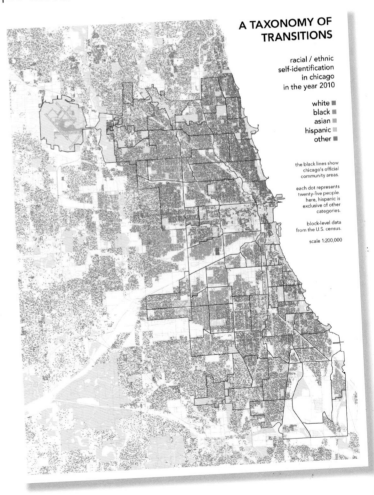

A TAXONOMY OF TRANSITIONS

racial / ethnic
self-identification
in chicago
in the year 2010

white ■
black ■
asian ■
hispanic ■
other ■

the black lines show
chicago's official
community areas.

each dot represents
twenty-five people.
here, hispanic is
exclusive of other
categories.

block-level data
from the U.S. census.

scale 1:200,000

Maps and Me

Plan Your Own Route

This map and satellite view both show the same section of Lower East Manhattan. Using the top map, plan a walking route from the subway station at Astor Place (M) to the subway station at 1st Avenue. Figure out the shortest route, or the route that takes you past places you might be interested in, such as movie theaters or restaurants. Then look at the satellite view of the same area. Which of these two maps do you think is easier to use and why? Does the satellite map give any other details that might be helpful in planning your journey?

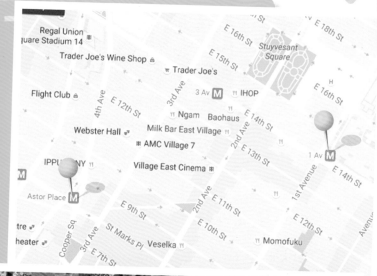

The amount of information needed to create a map of human activity can be huge. In modern mapmaking, information is usually processed using a **Geographic Information System** (GIS). These computer programs help convert statistical information or large **datasets** from the Internet into a form that can be displayed on a map.

Map (top) and satellite (bottom) views of Lower East Manhattan. The map leaves out detail included in the photograph. Do you think that makes it more or less informative?

HUMAN INTERACTIONS

One of the most difficult things to map is how people interact with one another. This is because human interactions are often very brief, and change all the time.

In many areas, census information helps mapmakers easily map where people live. Mapmakers use different ways to indicate how large or small cities and towns are. This may be as simple as using a bigger dot to mark cities with bigger populations. Cartographers have also found ways to measure and map how people move around. One way to measure this is by counting the number of people using roads or other forms of transportation such as railways, and figuring out the average number of travelers each day.

This map used mobile phone data to show common routes traveled in West Africa. These routes may show how the **ebola** disease spread.

FLOWMINDER.ORG

world pop

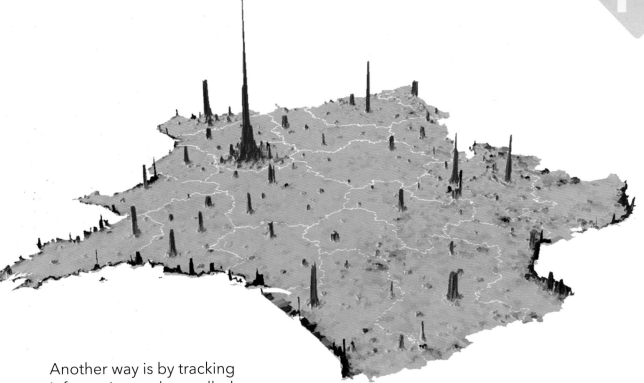

Another way is by tracking information such as cell-phone use. The **location services** that allow cell phones to use GPS technology also reveal where a phone is at any time. This information is often collected anonymously by phone providers.

Travel and Disease

One example of this type of location-service mapping came in 2014, when an **epidemic** of a disease called ebola broke out in West Africa. The disease was highly contagious, which means that it spread easily from person to person. The Swedish company Flowminder gathered information from 150,000 cell phones in the countries of Senegal, Guinea, and Liberia, to see how the disease may have spread.

When the data was put on a map, it showed a network of travel patterns across the region. Although the map did not track ebola itself, it showed the main routes people had traveled.

This map of France uses 3-D peaks to show where the populations in France are the highest during working periods (orange) and the holidays (blue).

Did You Know?

Flowminder is a company that uses maps to improve public health in poor countries. It uses billions of statistics to generate maps showing where people are in danger of disease or poverty.

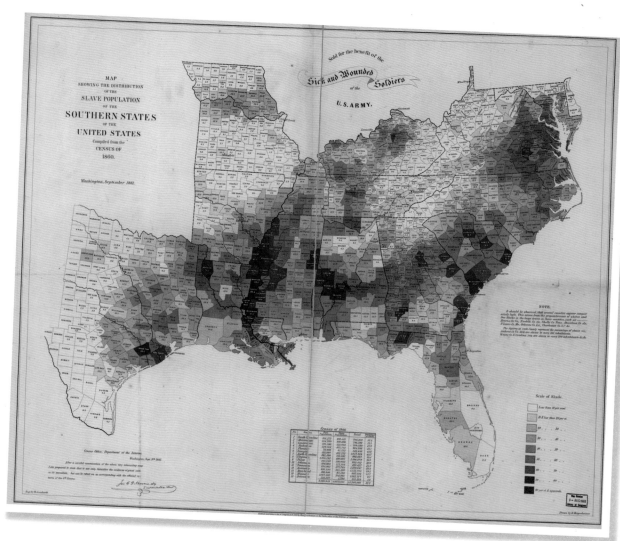

The information mapped by Flowminder helped health services to prevent the disease spreading further. The mapping process was similar to the one used by John Snow in 1854 to discover the source of cholera (see box, page 6).

After Snow's map, thematic mapping, or mapping information about a specific subject, had become common. In 1861, Edwin Hergesheimer drew a choropleth of the southern United States. He used shading to show the counties in the southern states with the highest **ratio** of slaves to nonslaves. The map showed how widespread slave labor was in almost all of the south.

Hergesheimer's map of slavery in the South was famous. President Abraham Lincoln even had the map included in one of his portraits.

This map by Eric Fischer uses data from walking sites on the Internet to map the most frequently walked routes in San Francisco.

Data Mapping

Data for modern thematic maps is often found on the Internet. Mapmaker Eric Fischer maps data about cities, such as favorite walking routes. In 2014, he gathered his information from details of walks that people posted online. Fischer's maps were an example of **crowd-sourced** mapping, in which details are collected anonymously from the Internet. This kind of mapping is also useful in real-time applications. It can tell people where there are available parking spots or show how busy public transportation is at any given time.

This Sanbourne map shows part of Richmond, Virginia, in 1905. Pink indicates brick buildings, and yellow shows wooden buildings.

Breakthroughs

Sanbourne Insurance Maps

In the 1800s, a remarkable series of maps was made by the Sanbourne Insurance Company in the United States. The company sold insurance to property owners. It needed to figure out the risk that a building might burn down. Sanbourne officals produced block-by-block maps of cities and towns. They color-coded every building to show its materials. Wooden buildings were most at risk of fire. As new buildings were constructed, the maps were updated.

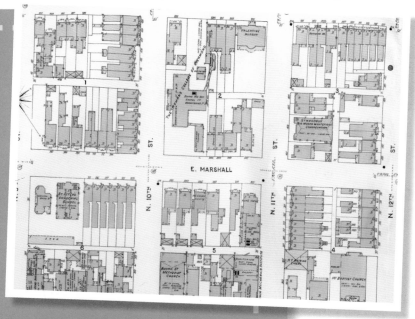

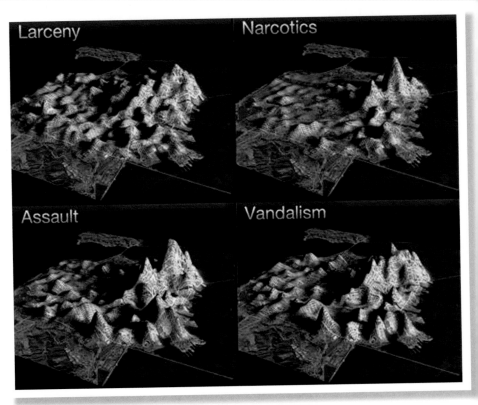

Larceny Narcotics

Assault Vandalism

Doug McCune used police figures to create 3-D maps of the occurrence of types of crime in San Francisco.

Mapping Crime

Crime is a human interaction that is often mapped, because it helps governments and law enforcement identify where the highest risks of crime are. To do so, mapmakers can use Geographic Information Systems to map police crime data. Mapmakers often mark areas where there is a risk of crime on a simple map.

In 2010, mapmaker Doug McCune mapped crime in San Francisco in a new way. He mapped incidents of crime in relief, or different heights shown in three dimensions (3D). The tallest peaks marked the most occurrences of a particular type of crime. The result is a series of different relief maps of San Francisco.

House Prices

Homebuyers often consult maps to determine where to buy a property. Realtors also use maps to help set the price of a property. Maps can show schools in an area, local crime figures, or the nearest parks. Some realtors figure out average travel times for people to go to work or school because they know that being close to good roads or public transit can raise real-estate values. This is an example where maps can have a direct impact on the price of a house.

Smell Maps

The artist Kate McLean maps cities according to their smells. She and other volunteers walk around and write down smells, from different types of take-out food to the smells of flowers or house paint. McLean then uses color coding to record the smells on a map. She believes that smell is closely linked to people's memories and emotions. She wants her maps to open a connection to an emotional side of life.

- Perfume
- Fast food outlets
- Wet moss
- Building dust
- Diesel fumes
- Carbolic soap
- Lorne (square) sausage
- Hot bovril at the footy
- River Clyde at low tide
- Subway

Glasgow's scents reflect the pride of its citizens, their ability to renew, regenerate and reinvent themselves and their buildings. Some scents illustrate the culture and geography of the city. The large dots represent the source of the smell and the smaller dots show their range and intensity. Glasgow's prevailing south-westerly wind causes the smells to mingle and drift across the city.

Negative Impressions

These types of crime maps are helpful to some people, such as the police, but they are not always welcomed by other people. A tourist organization, for example, might fear that this kind of map would make people less likely to want to visit their city or neighborhood. Realtors might also find it difficult to sell property in a particular neighborhood if it showed high incidences of crime.

Kate McLean created her smell map of Glasgow in 2014. It is an example of what she calls a **sensory** map.

HUMANS AND THE ENVIRONMENT

A key use of maps is to chart the location of valuable resources, and to record changes in the natural world that occur as a result of human interaction.

One of the earliest known maps was drawn in ancient Egypt about 3,100 years ago. It was on a sheet of papyrus. Papyrus is a paper-like material that was made from the fibers of a reed that grew along the banks of the River Nile. The map showed how to get to **quarries** in the desert. Stone from the quarries was a valuable resource in ancient Egypt. It was used to carve sculptures of the kings.

The Turin Papyrus is an ancient Egyptian map that shows routes to quarries in the desert.

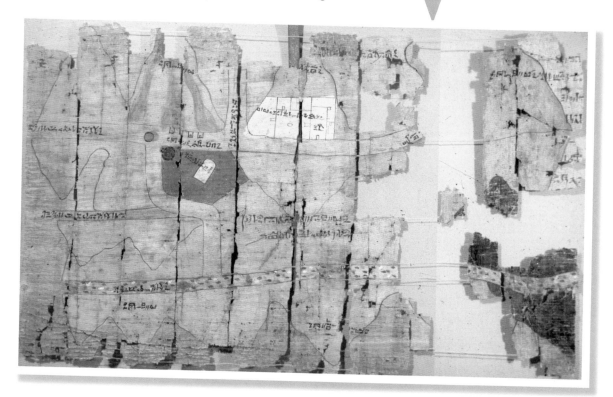

Looking for Resources

Today, people still use maps to chart the locations of resources around the world. For example, energy companies use maps of the **geological strata** beneath Earth's surface to figure out where they should drill for oil or natural gas. Often, these locations are in remote areas or beneath the bed of the ocean. It is important to pinpoint their exact location before any drilling begins.

Another use of maps is to record the changing natural environment. Maps help trace how human impact may be damaging the natural world. This helps governments and organizations to take steps to protect it. They might stop construction projects that will make rivers more likely to flood, for example.

This map uses color to show different rock formations in the state of Wyoming.

Recording Disaster

One important role of maps is to help predict natural disasters, such as earthquakes or floods, and lessen the damage they might cause. One way cartographers do this is to map the results of similar disasters in the past. This can reveal the areas most at risk from severe weather and damage from its effects. In many countries, for example, construction is limited on floodplains. These are natural areas that flood when rivers or other bodies of water overflow. They allow water to run off harmlessly. Building on them makes the effects of any floods far worse than before.

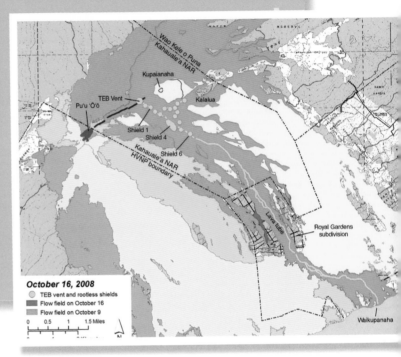

Surveying Earth

Since its launch in 1972, NASA's Landsat program has charted the impact of humans on the environment. A series of eight Landsat **satellites** have recorded Earth's surface. The satellites do not only take photographs. They also measure changes in the temperature of the atmosphere or changes in sea level or water temperature. This kind of data allows experts to measure changes in the environment, such as the way urbanization, or the expanding of cities, destroys natural habitats. The data can also show how pollution such as oil or sewage affects bodies of water or how smog, or air pollution, affects people living in cities. Because Landsat maps

This map shows the **lava** flows (pink and red) from a volcano that erupted in Hawaii in October 2008.

the same parts of the planet at regular intervals, it is useful for measuring environmental change over time.

One of the changes that most concerns experts is the rising of global sea levels. Experts fear that the rising temperature on Earth, caused by **climate change**, is causing the ice caps at the North and South Poles to melt. When the ice caps melt, the extra water causes sea levels around the world to rise. A rise of just a few feet in sea level would flood coastal communities in low-lying places such as the Maldives and Bangladesh. Careful mapping helps communities to understand where to build coastal defenses, such as dikes, to protect themselves.

This map shows the depth of flood waters in New Orleans a week after Hurricane Katrina in 2005. Red marks shallow flooding, yellow deeper waters, and green and blue the worst flooding.

Mapping Disaster

Mapping can also be useful to help with recovery after a natural disaster. In 2005, the city of New Orleans flooded after Hurricane Katrina.

The storm caused a rise in sea level and a tidal surge. Water overflowed the **levees**. The levees had been built to protect the low-lying city. Downtown New Orleans was devastated. More than 1,200 people died. Hundreds of thousands more were displaced from their flooded homes.

Exposing the Hidden

In the Amazon Rain Forest in Brazil, about 20 percent of the rain forest has been cut down in the last 40 years. This may damage Earth's ecosystem, because forests remove carbon dioxide (CO_2) from the atmosphere and turn it into oxygen. Humans need oxygen to breathe and depend on plants to create it. The Brazilian government has made some logging activity illegal. Some logging companies construct illegal roads and fell trees in secret in remote regions. The result of their activities is recorded by satellites in space.

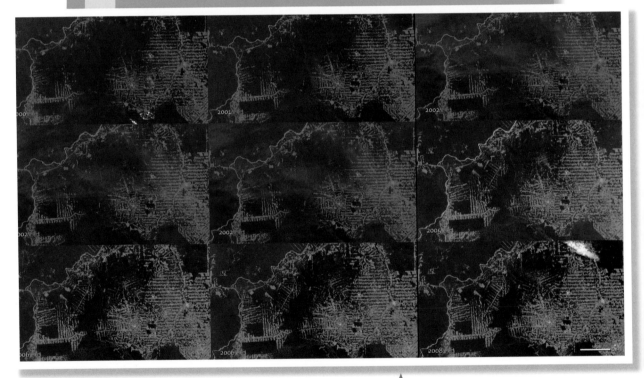

The flooding of New Orleans is one example of a natural disaster with devastating consequences for people. Maps are used to pinpoint places at risk of flooding, and to chart low lying areas along rivers and coasts. That helps governments and people living there to plan flood defenses.

These images from the Landsat satellite show annual deforestation in the same part of the Amazon over nine years.

Detecting Tsunamis

In the Indian Ocean, the Boxing Day **tsunami** of 2004 killed about 250,000 people. A system of detectors has now been put in place around the Indian Ocean. The detectors allow geographers to chart any movement of the seabed and predict the size, speed, and direction of any tsunami—and map where it may reach land. The early-warning system will allow governments to evacuate endangered areas around the coast more quickly than was possible before.

In the Real World

The Earth Observing System

NASA's Earth Observing System (EOS) is a collection of specialized satellites that constantly circle the planet. The role of EOS is to collect data on all parts of Earth's systems, from the water cycle to plant and animal life. EOS studies and maps climate change, the health of the ozone layer, natural disasters, pollution, plant growth, and the temperature of the oceans.

This map of the Indian Ocean tsunami shows the amplitude, or height, of waves from the highest (red) to the lowest (yellow and green).

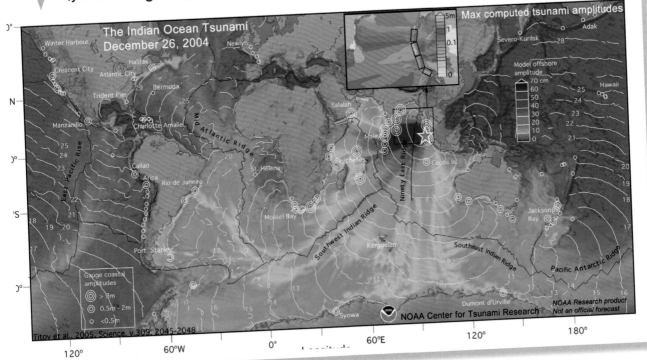

The Indian Ocean Tsunami
December 26, 2004

Max computed tsunami amplitudes

NOAA Center for Tsunami Research

MAPS AND TRAVEL

More people travel more often to more places than at any time in the past. Modern technology means that they should never get lost—at least in theory.

In the modern world, everyone is familiar with electronic maps on smartphones, tablets, or navigation devices. These maps use the global positioning system (GPS) to help the user to navigate. GPS satellites track the user's location. The device then combines this information with a database of maps to plot a route to the user's destination and to direct him or her along the route. The device can show progress on a map and give written or spoken directions about which route to take at any intersections.

This U.S. map used tracking systems on ships to record the prominence of commercial shipping along the East Coast.

A cyclist uses a GPS display on a cellphone to plan a route.

Constant live updates of the GPS allows maps to automatically show areas of construction or congestion, or traffic accidents, and prompt drivers to take a detour. The system can also calculate the shortest route for drivers or pedestrians, and direct them away from highways or roads with tolls, or fees.

GPS for Personal Use

The GPS system also allows individuals to generate personal maps. People can store previous routes, which means that runners or cyclists, for example, can track their own activity. The system calculates average speeds and records, and route details such as distance, direction, and elevation, or how much land rises or falls. Users can share their routes with other users, or search for other people's routes when they are visiting a new location.

Did You Know?

The GPS system consists of 24 satellites in orbit above Earth. A minimum of four satellites are usually in view of any point on the planet. This means they are detectable by tracking devices, not that they are visible to the human eye.

シベリア

北京
大連
東京
香港
太平洋

デ・・・

Similar GPS technology is usually available for air travelers. They can follow the Skymap from their seats, so they can see the exact progress a flight is making. Friends or relatives can log on to flight-tracking websites and see exactly where their visitors are. Pilots have far more detailed maps. Each airport has guide maps showing the direction of take-off and the angle at which the plane will descend, or fly to the ground.

Transmitters placed all around an airport constantly **triangulate** the positions of airplanes. They can report the position of a plane to both the pilot in the cockpit and the air traffic controllers. Airplanes still carry paper charts for pilots. They are used in emergencies in case eletronic systems fail.

Air passengers around the world can follow their journey from their seat using a GPS flight tracker. This Japanese flight is approaching Japan over eastern Russia.

This **portolan** from the 1300s shows the names of ports around the Mediterranean Sea. The lines are to help sailors plan their course.

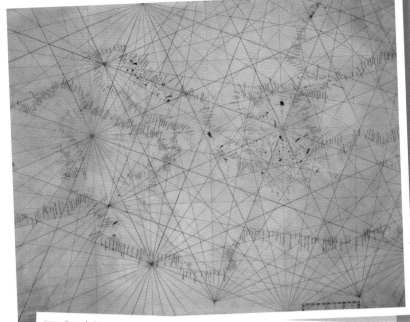

Travel at Sea

Some of the earliest travel maps were designed for sailors. Portolans were used in the 1300s. They had **bearing lines** connecting ports, or the places where ships would dock. The lines helped sailors at sea to plot a direct course.

These early portolans reduced the information on a map to an outline of the coast and a list of the ports along it. The lines on the maps were straight, because ships at sea can sail in straight lines. Today, detailed maps of ports have markings that tell sailors how deep the water is in different areas. They indicate safe channels between rocks, ships, and hazards such as sandbanks. In recent decades, most marine charts are digital. They give sailors a precise location. Digitization also allows charts to be regularly updated to show any hazards that may have have moved.

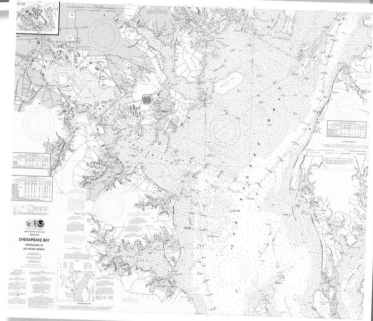

This modern sea chart shows routes and obstacles in Chesapeake Bay for ships heading to Baltimore Harbor.

Maps and Tourism

Most visitors to a new place need some kind of map to guide them around. Many tourist maps feature small drawings or photographs of popular attractions. They do not feature the rest of the city, because tourists are usually interested in only the major sites. Some maps help encourage tourists to visit a particular place. Rather than showing the locations of different tourist attractions, this kind of map displays a place in the most attractive way possible. It might emphasize certain features, and may look more like paintings than regular maps. How do you think this map differs from a regular street map? If you were a tourist, would you want to visit the park?

A Revolutionary Map

Many maps today are similar to the early portolans, which show straight lines and only the most important information. In some ways they are more like diagrams than maps. The first modern example of this was the London Underground map drawn by Harry Beck in 1933. His map laid out the London subway system in a clear, useful way. Beck showed only information travelers needed, not the precise route of the lines.

Heinrich Berann painted this panoramic map of Yellowstone National Park in 1962. The map was intended to encourage visitors to the park.

The map Beck drew is useful to travelers because they only need to know when the subway is reaching their stop, and where they can change subway routes to reach their destinations. They did not need to know the real route of the tracks or the exact distances between stations. Beck's map remains the basis of modern London Underground maps.

This map of the Metrorail System in Detroit follows the same method as Harry Beck's original London Underground map in 1933.

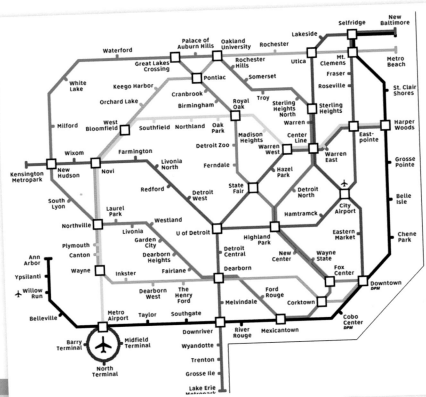

Breakthroughs

Transit Maps

Harry Beck's map of the London Underground set the approach for nearly all future maps of mass-transit systems. Modern mass-transit maps use bright colors to display routes, and the lines on the map follow simpler routes than the routes actually follow in real life. These maps also ignore the real distances between stations or bus stops, because travelers only need to know the order in which stops occur. Mass-transit maps use clear lettering for station names. This makes it easier for travelers to read small, folding versions of the map as they travel.

MAPS IN YOUR WORLD

There are many different ways to map your own activity in your local community. Whatever map you create reflects your personality and choices.

How would you go about mapping activity in your life? There are many different ways to map your local town or the places you visit. You could draw a map of your neighborhood showing things you are interested in, such as shopping malls, sports fields, or parks. Or you could track your own movements and activities on a map. Maybe you could color code them to show the type of thing you were doing, or use different lines and symbols to mean different things. Make sure you use a key to show what each color or symbol represents. However you make your map, it will be unique to you.

This map of part of Manhattan is formed from a collage of other maps from take-out restaurants and other leaflets. Could you make a collage of your town from local maps?

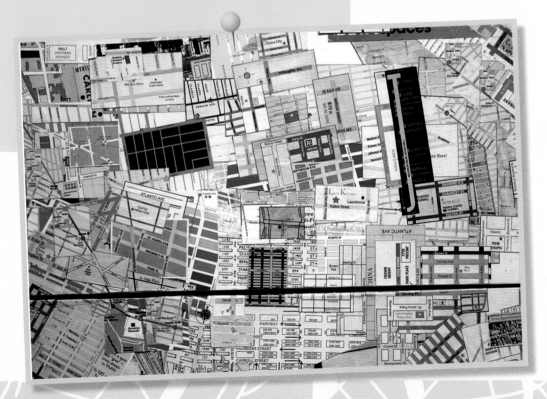

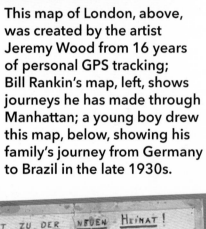

foot
train
car

friend
activity
restaurant
bar

This map of London, above, was created by the artist Jeremy Wood from 16 years of personal GPS tracking; Bill Rankin's map, left, shows journeys he has made through Manhattan; a young boy drew this map, below, showing his family's journey from Germany to Brazil in the late 1930s.

All three maps on this page show an image of a personal journey. They were all created in different ways. Which of these maps do you find most interesting?

Glossary

bearing lines Lines that follow the major directions on a compass, such as north, northeast, or east, to help people plan a route

cartographers People who make and study maps

census An official count and survey of the population of a country

choropleth A map in which areas are shaded to convey information

climate change The impact of humans on Earth's climate, making it warmer

crowd-sourced Describes information gained from large numbers of people, usually online

data Facts and statistics

datasets Large collections of data

distribution The way in which something is spread out among a group or over an area

ebola A deadly and very contagious virus

epidemic A widespread outbreak of an infectious disease

ethnicity Describing a certain group with a common racial, national, social, cultural, or religious background

Geographic Information Systems Computer programs that use a wide range of sources to generate maps

geological Relating to the rocks that make up the Earth

Global Positioning System A network of satellites used to provide location information

lava Molten rock

levees Earth banks that prevent a river from flooding

literacy The ability to read and write

location services Apps that identify the location of portable devices

minimum The least amount possible

ozone layer A layer of gas high in the atmosphere that protects Earth from harmful radiation in space

portolan An early sea chart

quarries Pits where stone is dug

race Usually defined as a division of people in the human population that have similar physical characteristics, coming from a common ancestry

ratio The relation between two numbers

relief Showing different heights

resources Things that can be used for a specific purpose

satellites Artificial bodies that orbit Earth in order to collect information

sensory Related to the five senses

social reformers People who try to make improvements in the daily lives of poor people

statistics Large quantities of numerical data

strata The layers of rock that make up the Earth

triangulate To pinpoint a location by using math and the distance to two known locations

tsunami A large wave caused by an earthquake beneath the ocean

visualize To form an image of something in one's mind

On the Web

www.canadiangeographic.ca/kids
A site where children can learn about their world with fun facts, kids games, and an interactive map.

www.nationalgeographic.com/kids-world-atlas/maps.html
National Geographic's site allows kids to create their own maps.

http://www.flowminder.org/
The site of Flowminder, which uses maps to chart poverty and disease in undeveloped countries.

https://www.openstreetmap.org/#map=5/51.500/-0.100
OpenStreetMap is a digital world map created and added to by volunteers. Get involved and help map your local area.

http://www.missingmaps.org/
A site that encourages people to map things that do not normally get mapped. Learn how to create your own maps—you may need help from an adult.

Books

Berry, Jill K, and Linden McNeilly. *Map Art Lab: 52 Exciting Explorations in Mapmaking, Imagination, and Travel.* Lab Series. Quarry Books, 2014.

National Geographic Kids World Atlas. National Geographic Children's, 2013.

Panchyk, Richard. *Charting the World: Geography and Maps from Cave Paintings to GPS with 21 Activities.* Chicago Review, 2011.

Peetoom, Laura, and Paul Heersink. *Maps and Mapping for Canadian Kids.* Scholastic Canada, 2011.

Index